# Table of Contents

# Part 1:

# Observability and Management

# Monitoring and Logging

## Prometheus and Grafana

When managing Kubernetes clusters, **Prometheus** and **Grafana** are commonly used together to monitor and visualize the system's performance, health, and behaviour. Here's a breakdown of how they work and integrate effectively in a Kubernetes environment.

### 1. Prometheus in Kubernetes

#### What is Prometheus?

Prometheus is an open-source monitoring and alerting system built for cloud-native environments. It collects metrics, stores them in a time-series database, and enables users to query and alert based on those metrics.

#### How Prometheus Works in Kubernetes

- **Data Collection:** Prometheus scrapes metrics from endpoints exposed by Kubernetes pods, nodes, and services.
- **Service Discovery:** Prometheus automatically discovers services and endpoints in a Kubernetes cluster using Kubernetes APIs. It dynamically adjusts to changes in the environment.
- **Time-Series Database:** All collected metrics are stored with timestamps in a time-series database.

- **Alerting System:** Prometheus has an alert manager that triggers alerts based on defined rules.

**Prometheus Architecture in Kubernetes**

- **Prometheus Server:** Collects, stores, and processes data.
- **Exporters:** Export application or system metrics in a format that Prometheus can scrape.
    - Example: node_exporter, kube-state-metrics
- **Service Discovery:** Automatically finds new services in the cluster.
- **Alertmanager:** Sends notifications when alert conditions are met.
- **Storage:** Stores time-series data efficiently for querying.

**How Prometheus Scrapes Metrics in Kubernetes**

1. **Kubernetes Service Discovery:** Prometheus queries the Kubernetes API to discover pods, services, and endpoints.
2. **Endpoints Exposure:** Applications expose /metrics endpoints via HTTP. Common libraries (like Prometheus client for Go, Python, Java) are used to expose custom application metrics.
3. **Scraping Configuration:** Configured via a prometheus.yml file. Scraping intervals and targets are defined.

```
scrape_configs:
  - job_name: 'kubernetes-nodes'
    kubernetes_sd_configs:
      - role: node
    scheme: https
    tls_config:
      insecure_skip_verify: true
```

**2. Grafana in Kubernetes**

**What is Grafana?**

Grafana is an open-source visualization platform that provides interactive dashboards for metrics, logs, and traces. It connects with multiple data sources (like Prometheus) and transforms the data into visually appealing graphs and panels.

### How Grafana Works in Kubernetes

- **Data Source Connection:** Grafana connects to Prometheus as a data source using HTTP.
- **Querying Metrics:** Users can create custom queries using PromQL (Prometheus Query Language) or other query languages.
- **Building Dashboards:** Grafana provides an easy-to-use interface to create, share, and manage dashboards.
- **Alerting System:** Similar to Prometheus, Grafana can be configured to send alerts when specified thresholds are breached.

### Grafana Architecture in Kubernetes

- **Grafana Server:** Handles API requests, user management, and dashboard rendering.
- **Data Source Plugin:** Connects to Prometheus or other systems.
- **Storage:** Stores dashboard and user data (usually in a database like SQLite, MySQL, or PostgreSQL).
- **UI/UX Interface:** Allows users to create and manage visualizations and dashboards.

## 3. Deploying Prometheus and Grafana in Kubernetes

### Step 1: Install Prometheus Using Helm

Helm is a popular package manager for Kubernetes.

```
# Add Prometheus Helm repo
helm repo add prometheus-community https://prometheus-community.github.io/helm-charts

# Install Prometheus
helm install prometheus prometheus-community/Prometheus
```

### Step 2: Install Grafana Using Helm

```
# Add Grafana Helm repo
helm repo add grafana https://grafana.github.io/helm-charts
```

```
# Install Grafana
helm install grafana grafana/Grafana
```

**Step 3: Configure Prometheus as a Data Source in Grafana**

1. Access Grafana via NodePort or Ingress.
2. Log in using default credentials (admin/admin).
3. Go to Configuration -> Data Sources -> Add Data Source.
4. Select Prometheus and configure:
   - URL: http://prometheus-server:9090
   - Save and Test.

### 4. Integration Between Prometheus and Grafana

- **Prometheus Scrapes Metrics:** Collects data from Kubernetes nodes, pods, and services.
- **Grafana Queries Prometheus:** Grafana uses PromQL to query and visualize this data.
- **Dashboards and Alerts:** Grafana presents the data through customized dashboards and triggers alerts when necessary.

### 5. Common Use Cases

- **Cluster Health Monitoring:** CPU, memory, and resource usage.
- **Application Performance:** Track latency, request counts, and error rates.
- **Alerting and Incident Response:** Notify when critical thresholds are breached.
- **Custom Business Metrics:** Track user activities, orders, and other business KPIs.

### 6. Key Benefits of Using Prometheus and Grafana

- **Scalability:** Handles dynamic Kubernetes environments efficiently.
- **Real-Time Monitoring:** Provides up-to-date insights into system performance.
- **Customizable Visualizations:** Create tailored dashboards for different audiences.
- **Open-Source and Extensible:** Easily extendable with exporters and plugins.

**7. Advanced Configurations**

- **Prometheus Federation:** Scale monitoring across multiple clusters.
- **Grafana Provisioning:** Automate dashboard creation and data source management.
- **Alerting with Alertmanager and Grafana:** Combine alerts from both systems for reliability.

**8. Final Thoughts**

Prometheus and Grafana together provide a powerful monitoring and visualization solution for Kubernetes. Prometheus efficiently collects and processes metrics, while Grafana transforms that data into actionable insights, ensuring smooth cluster operations and improving overall system reliability.

# Fluentd, ElasticSearch, Kibana

Here's a detailed breakdown of **Fluentd, Elasticsearch, and Kibana (EFK Stack)** in a **Kubernetes** environment, with explanations and relevant YAML manifests.

**Objective:**

Set up centralized logging in Kubernetes using the

**EFK stack**:

- **Fluentd**: Collect and forward logs.
- **Elasticsearch**: Store and index logs.
- **Kibana**: Visualize and analyze logs.

**1. Fluentd**

**Purpose:**

- Fluentd collects logs from Kubernetes pods and nodes, formats them, and forwards them to Elasticsearch.

- It uses Kubernetes metadata to enrich the logs.

**Fluentd Configuration:**

Fluentd is configured using a ConfigMap that defines its behavior. Below is a basic fluentd-configmap.yaml:

```
apiVersion: v1
kind: ConfigMap
metadata:
  name: fluentd-config
  namespace: kube-system
data:
  fluent.conf: |
    <source>
      @type tail
      path /var/log/containers/*.log
      pos_file /var/log/fluentd-containers.log.pos
      tag kubernetes.*
      read_from_head true
      <parse>
        @type json
        time_key time
        time_format %Y-%m-%dT%H:%M:%S.%NZ
      </parse>
    </source>

    <filter kubernetes.**>
      @type kubernetes_metadata
    </filter>

    <match **>
      @type elasticsearch
      host elasticsearch
      port 9200
      logstash_format true
      logstash_prefix kubernetes
      logstash_dateformat %Y.%m.%d
      flush_interval 5s
    </match>
```

**Fluentd DaemonSet:**

Fluentd runs as a DaemonSet to ensure it is deployed on all nodes.

```
apiVersion: apps/v1
```

```yaml
kind: DaemonSet
metadata:
  name: fluentd
  namespace: kube-system
  labels:
    k8s-app: fluentd
spec:
  selector:
    matchLabels:
      name: fluentd
  template:
    metadata:
      labels:
        name: fluentd
    spec:
      containers:
        - name: fluentd
          image: fluent/fluentd:v1.14.2
          env:
            - name: FLUENTD_CONF
              value: fluent.conf
          volumeMounts:
            - name: config-volume
              mountPath: /fluentd/etc/
            - name: varlog
              mountPath: /var/log
      volumes:
        - name: config-volume
          configMap:
            name: fluentd-config
        - name: varlog
          hostPath:
            path: /var/log
```

**2. Elasticsearch**

**Purpose:**

- Elasticsearch stores logs and makes them searchable.
- It indexes logs received from Fluentd.

**Elasticsearch Deployment:**

```yaml
apiVersion: apps/v1
kind: StatefulSet
metadata:
```

```
 name: elasticsearch
 namespace: kube-system
spec:
 serviceName: elasticsearch
 replicas: 1
 selector:
  matchLabels:
   app: elasticsearch
 template:
  metadata:
   labels:
    app: elasticsearch
  spec:
   containers:
    - name: elasticsearch
     image:
docker.elastic.co/elasticsearch/elasticsearch:7.15.0
     ports:
      - containerPort: 9200
     env:
      - name: discovery.type
       value: "single-node"
      - name: ES_JAVA_OPTS
       value: "-Xms512m -Xmx512m"
     volumeMounts:
      - name: data
       mountPath: /usr/share/elasticsearch/data
   volumes:
    - name: data
     emptyDir: {}
```

**Elasticsearch Service:**

```
apiVersion: v1
kind: Service
metadata:
 name: elasticsearch
 namespace: kube-system
spec:
 selector:
  app: elasticsearch
 ports:
  - port: 9200
   targetPort: 9200
```

**3. Kibana**

**Purpose:**

- Kibana provides a web interface to query, visualize, and analyze logs stored in Elasticsearch.

**Kibana Deployment:**

```
apiVersion: apps/v1
kind: Deployment
metadata:
  name: kibana
  namespace: kube-system
spec:
  replicas: 1
  selector:
    matchLabels:
      app: kibana
  template:
    metadata:
      labels:
        app: kibana
    spec:
      containers:
        - name: kibana
          image: docker.elastic.co/kibana/kibana:7.15.0
          env:
            - name: ELASTICSEARCH_HOSTS
              value: "http://elasticsearch:9200"
          ports:
            - containerPort: 5601
```

**Kibana Service:**

```
apiVersion: v1
kind: Service
metadata:
  name: kibana
  namespace: kube-system
spec:
  type: NodePort
  selector:
    app: kibana
  ports:
    - port: 5601
      targetPort: 5601
      nodePort: 30000
```

## 4. Deploying the EFK Stack

### Step 1: Apply Configs

```
kubectl apply -f fluentd-configmap.yaml
kubectl apply -f fluentd-daemonset.yaml
kubectl apply -f elasticsearch.yaml
kubectl apply -f elasticsearch-service.yaml
kubectl apply -f kibana.yaml
kubectl apply -f kibana-service.yaml
```

### Step 2: Access Kibana

- Get the Kibana NodePort:

```
kubectl get svc kibana -n kube-system
```

- Access Kibana via:
  Cpp:

```
http://<NODE_IP>:30000
```

## 5. Visualizing Logs in Kibana

### Create Index Pattern:

1. Open Kibana.
2. Navigate to **Management > Index Patterns**.
3. Create a new index pattern with kubernetes-*.
4. Select @timestamp as the time field.

## 6. Debugging & Troubleshooting

- Check logs for Fluentd:

```
kubectl logs <fluentd-pod> -n kube-system
```

- Check Elasticsearch health:

```
kubectl exec -it <elasticsearch-pod> -n kube-system
-- curl -XGET 'localhost:9200/_cluster/health?pretty'
```

- Check Kibana:

```
kubectl logs <kibana-pod> -n kube-system
```

You now have a fully functional **EFK stack** to capture, store, and analyze Kubernetes logs. If you need advanced features like alerting or security, you can enhance this stack by configuring the Elastic Stack further.

# Kubernetes Debugging with kubectl

Debugging in Kubernetes involves identifying and fixing issues with pods, containers, services, and other Kubernetes resources. Using kubectl, you can diagnose and troubleshoot cluster issues effectively.

**Goal:**

- Identify and fix issues in Kubernetes using kubectl commands.
- Debug pods, containers, and nodes.
- Investigate application logs and network problems.

### 1. Debugging Kubernetes Pods

#### A. Check Pod Status

To identify the status of pods and detect errors.

kubectl get pods -n <namespace>

Example:

kubectl get pods -n my-app

Look at the STATUS column:

- Pending – Pod is waiting for resources.
- ContainerCreating – Container is starting.
- CrashLoopBackOff – Container is repeatedly crashing.
- ImagePullBackOff – Issues pulling container image.

#### B. Describe Pod to Get More Details

kubectl describe pod <pod-name> -n <namespace>

Example:

kubectl describe pod my-app-pod -n my-app

- Check **Events** section for failures (e.g., image pull errors, liveness probe failures).

**C. Check Pod Logs**

View logs for a specific container in a pod.

kubectl logs <pod-name> -n <namespace> --container <container-name>

Example:

kubectl logs my-app-pod -n my-app --container my-container

- Add -f to follow the logs in real-time:

  kubectl logs my-app-pod -n my-app -f

**D. Get Logs from Previous Container Restart**

kubectl logs <pod-name> -n <namespace> --previous

Example:

kubectl logs my-app-pod -n my-app –previous

Useful for debugging **CrashLoopBackOff** errors.

**E. Open a Shell into a Running Container**

To run shell commands inside a running pod.

kubectl exec -it <pod-name> -n <namespace> -- /bin/sh

Example:

kubectl exec -it my-app-pod -n my-app -- /bin/sh

For a pod with multiple containers:

kubectl exec -it <pod-name> -n <namespace> -c <container-name> -- /bin/sh

- If the container uses bash:

  kubectl exec -it my-app-pod -n my-app -- /bin/bash

**2. Debugging Container Issues**

**A. Check Container Logs**

kubectl logs <pod-name> -c <container-name> -n <namespace>

Example:

kubectl logs my-app-pod -c my-container -n my-app

**B. Get Container Environment Variables**

kubectl exec -it <pod-name> -n <namespace> -- env

Example:

kubectl exec -it my-app-pod -n my-app – env

**C. Run Commands Inside Container**

kubectl exec -it <pod-name> -n <namespace> -- <command>

Example:

kubectl exec -it my-app-pod -n my-app -- ls /app

**3. Debugging Failed Pods**

**A. Identify Crash Reason**

Check the reason for container restarts.

kubectl get pods -n <namespace>

Look for CrashLoopBackOff or Error.

**B. Describe Pod to Check Events**

kubectl describe pod <pod-name> -n <namespace>

Example:

kubectl describe pod my-app-pod -n my-app

Check the **Events** section for detailed error messages.

**4. Debugging Network Issues**

**A. Check Service Configuration**

kubectl get svc -n <namespace>

**Example:**

kubectl get svc -n my-app

**B. Describe Service for Details**

kubectl describe svc <service-name> -n <namespace>

Example:

kubectl describe svc my-app-service -n my-app

**C. Test Internal Connectivity Using BusyBox**

kubectl run busybox --image=busybox --restart=Never -it -- /bin/sh

# Check DNS resolution
nslookup my-app-service

# Test connectivity to the service
wget my-app-service:8080

**5. Debugging Node Issues**

**A. Check Node Status**

kubectl get nodes

Example:

kubectl get nodes

**B. Describe Node for More Info**

kubectl describe node <node-name>

Example:

kubectl describe node node-1

- Check for taints, disk pressure, and resource limits.

**C. Check Node Logs**

kubectl logs <pod-name> -n <namespace> --previous

- Check kubelet logs:

  journalctl -u kubelet

- Check Docker or container runtime logs:

  journalctl -u docker

**6. Using kubectl debug for Troubleshooting**

**A. Create a Debug Pod with an Ephemeral Container**

If the pod is running, but the main container cannot be accessed, use an ephemeral debug container.

kubectl debug <pod-name> -n <namespace> --image=busybox --target=<container-name>

Example:

kubectl debug my-app-pod -n my-app --image=busybox --target=my-container

**B. Debugging Node with Privileged Container**

kubectl debug node/<node-name> -it --image=busybox

Example:

kubectl debug node/node-1 -it --image=busybox

**7. Advanced Debugging Techniques**

**A. Port Forwarding for Service Debugging**

kubectl port-forward svc/<service-name> <local-port>:<service-port> -n <namespace>

**Example:**

kubectl port-forward svc/my-app-service 8080:80 -n my-app

Access the service at:

http://localhost:8080

### B. Copy Files from/into a Pod

# Copy from pod to local
kubectl cp <namespace>/<pod-name>:/path/to/file /local/path

# Copy from local to pod
kubectl cp /local/path <namespace>/<pod-name>:/path/to/file

Example:

kubectl cp my-app/my-app-pod:/app/logs.txt ./logs.txt

## 8. Debugging Deployment Failures

### A. Check Deployment Status

kubectl get deploy -n <namespace>

Example:

kubectl get deploy -n my-app

### B. Describe Deployment for Details

kubectl describe deploy <deployment-name> -n <namespace>

**Example:**

kubectl describe deploy my-app-deployment -n my-app

## 9. Debugging StatefulSets and DaemonSets

### A. Check StatefulSet Status

kubectl get statefulsets -n <namespace>

**B. Check DaemonSet Status**

kubectl get daemonsets -n <namespace>

**10. Final Tips for Debugging Kubernetes**

- Use kubectl get and kubectl describe to get insights into resource statuses.
- Always check pod/container logs to identify application-level errors.
- Debug network connectivity with busybox or curl inside a pod.
- Test service reachability using kubectl port-forward.
- Debug nodes for resource pressure or kernel issues if pods are evicted or stuck.

# Autoscaling and Optimization

## Horizontal and Vertical Pod Autoscalers

**Kubernetes Autoscaling: Horizontal and Vertical Pod Autoscalers (HPA & VPA)**

Autoscaling in Kubernetes ensures that applications handle varying loads effectively by adjusting the number of pods or the resources allocated to them dynamically.

**Goal:**

- Automatically adjust pod replicas based on CPU, memory, or custom metrics.
- Increase or decrease pod resource requests and limits dynamically.

### 1. Introduction to Autoscaling

#### Horizontal Pod Autoscaler (HPA)

- Increases or decreases the **number of pods** based on CPU, memory, or custom metrics.
- Example: Scale pods from 1 to 10 based on 70% CPU usage.

#### Vertical Pod Autoscaler (VPA)

- Adjusts **CPU and memory requests/limits** for individual pods dynamically.
- Ensures pods get appropriate resources without manual intervention.

### 2. Horizontal Pod Autoscaler (HPA)

#### How HPA Works

- Monitors CPU, memory, or custom metrics.
- Automatically scales the number of pods up or down based on threshold values.
- Useful for stateless applications that can scale horizontally.

**Step 1: Create a Sample Deployment**

```
apiVersion: apps/v1
kind: Deployment
metadata:
  name: my-app
  namespace: default
  labels:
    app: my-app
spec:
  replicas: 1
  selector:
    matchLabels:
      app: my-app
```

```
  template:
    metadata:
      labels:
        app: my-app
    spec:
      containers:
        - name: my-app
          image: nginx
          resources:
            requests:
              cpu: "200m"
              memory: "256Mi"
            limits:
              cpu: "500m"
              memory: "512Mi"
          ports:
            - containerPort: 80
```

```
kubectl apply -f my-app-deployment.yaml
```

**Step 2: Create Horizontal Pod Autoscaler (HPA)**

```
# Create HPA with 70% CPU utilization target
kubectl autoscale deployment my-app --cpu-percent=70 --min=1 --max=10
```

OR Define HPA in a YAML file:

```
apiVersion: autoscaling/v2
kind: HorizontalPodAutoscaler
metadata:
  name: my-app-hpa
  namespace: default
spec:
  scaleTargetRef:
    apiVersion: apps/v1
    kind: Deployment
    name: my-app
  minReplicas: 1
  maxReplicas: 10
  metrics:
    - type: Resource
      resource:
        name: cpu
        target:
          type: Utilization
          averageUtilization: 70
```

kubectl apply -f my-app-hpa.yaml

**Step 3: Verify HPA Configuration**

kubectl get hpa

Expected Output:

NAME REFERENCE TARGETS MINPODS MAXPODS REPLICAS AGE
my-app-hpa Deployment/my-app 50%/70% 1 10 3 10m

**Step 4: Test HPA**

To generate load and test scaling:

kubectl run -i --tty load-generator --image=busybox -- /bin/sh
# Inside the busybox shell
while true; do wget -q -O- http://my-app.default.svc.cluster.local; done

Check updated HPA state:

kubectl get hpa

**3. Vertical Pod Autoscaler (VPA)**

**How VPA Works**

- Dynamically adjusts **CPU and memory requests/limits** for containers.
- Ensures that pods use the right amount of resources.
- Best for workloads that scale vertically.

---

**Step 1: Install VPA using Helm**

```
# Add VPA helm repo
helm repo add fairwinds-stable https://charts.fairwinds.com/stable
helm repo update

# Install VPA
helm install vpa fairwinds-stable/vpa
```

**Step 2: Create VPA for Deployment**

Define my-app-vpa.yaml:

```yaml
apiVersion: autoscaling.k8s.io/v1
kind: VerticalPodAutoscaler
metadata:
  name: my-app-vpa
  namespace: default
spec:
  targetRef:
    apiVersion: apps/v1
    kind: Deployment
    name: my-app
  updatePolicy:
    updateMode: "Auto"  # Options: Auto, Off, Initial
  resourcePolicy:
    containerPolicies:
      - containerName: my-app
        minAllowed:
          cpu: "100m"
          memory: "128Mi"
        maxAllowed:
          cpu: "1"
          memory: "1Gi"
        controlledResources: ["cpu", "memory"]
```

```
kubectl apply -f my-app-vpa.yaml
```

**Update Modes:**

- Auto – Automatically apply recommended values.
- Initial – Apply recommendations only on pod creation.
- Off – Only show recommendations without applying them.

**Step 3: Verify VPA Status**

```
kubectl describe vpa my-app-vpa
```

Expected Output:

```
Recommendations:
  Target:
    Cpu:     250m
    Memory:  400Mi
```

**Step 4: Check VPA Recommendations**

```
kubectl get vpa
```

Check the recommendations:

```
kubectl describe vpa my-app-vpa
```

## 4. Comparing HPA and VPA

| Feature | HPA | VPA |
|---|---|---|
| Scaling Strategy | Horizontal (number of pods) | Vertical (resource limits) |
| Metrics | CPU, memory, custom | CPU and memory |
| Use Case | Stateless apps | Stateful apps, resource-intensive workloads |
| Response Time | Fast | Slower |
| Potential Conflicts | Yes (when combined with VPA) | No conflicts |

## 5. Combining HPA and VPA (Advanced)

You can use HPA and VPA together but with some restrictions:

- **HPA:** Scales the number of pods.
- **VPA:** Adjusts resource requests and limits.
- **Best Practice:** Use HPA to scale pods and set VPA in off mode for recommendations only.

**Example: Configure HPA and VPA Together**

```
apiVersion: autoscaling/v2
kind: HorizontalPodAutoscaler
metadata:
  name: my-app-hpa
  namespace: default
spec:
  scaleTargetRef:
    apiVersion: apps/v1
    kind: Deployment
    name: my-app
```

```yaml
  minReplicas: 1
  maxReplicas: 10
  metrics:
    - type: Resource
      resource:
        name: cpu
        target:
          type: Utilization
          averageUtilization: 70
---
apiVersion: autoscaling.k8s.io/v1
kind: VerticalPodAutoscaler
metadata:
  name: my-app-vpa
  namespace: default
spec:
  targetRef:
    apiVersion: apps/v1
    kind: Deployment
    name: my-app
  updatePolicy:
    updateMode: "Off"  # Avoid conflicts with HPA
```

**6. Monitoring Autoscaling**

**A. Monitor HPA**

```
kubectl get hpa
```

**B. Monitor VPA Recommendations**

```
kubectl describe vpa my-app-vpa
```

**7. Troubleshooting Autoscaling**

**Check HPA Events**

```
kubectl describe hpa my-app-hpa
```

**Check VPA Recommendations**

```
kubectl describe vpa my-app-vpa
```

**Logs for Autoscaler Components**

```
kubectl logs -n kube-system -l app=metrics-server
```

**Check Pod/Node Utilization**

```
kubectl top pods
kubectl top nodes
```

**8. Recap**

- **HPA** scales pods horizontally to handle increased load.
- **VPA** automatically adjusts resource requests and limits to optimize performance.
- Use HPA and VPA carefully together to avoid conflicts.

Now you're ready to dynamically scale and optimize your Kubernetes workloads!

# Cluster Autoscaler in Kubernetes

Cluster Autoscaler (CA) is a Kubernetes component that automatically scales the number of nodes in a cluster based on workload demands. It adds nodes when Pods fail to schedule due to resource constraints and removes underutilized nodes to optimize costs.

**How Cluster Autoscaler Works**

**1. Scaling Up (Adding Nodes)**

- When a Pod cannot be scheduled due to insufficient CPU or memory, CA detects this.
- It communicates with the cloud provider to add nodes to the cluster.
- Once the new nodes are available, Kubernetes schedules the pending Pods.

**2. Scaling Down (Removing Nodes)**

- CA identifies underutilized nodes.
- It ensures Pods on those nodes can be rescheduled elsewhere.

- If a node is mostly empty for a defined period, it gets removed.

**Cluster Autoscaler Setup**

**1. Prerequisites**

- A Kubernetes cluster running on a cloud provider that supports autoscaling (AWS, GCP, Azure, etc.).
- kubectl configured for cluster access.
- Cluster Autoscaler deployed.

**2. Installing Cluster Autoscaler**

You deploy CA as a Deployment in your cluster. Below is a Deployment YAML for CA in an AWS EKS cluster:
**Cluster Autoscaler Deployment (AWS EKS)**

```
apiVersion: apps/v1
kind: Deployment
metadata:
  name: cluster-autoscaler
  namespace: kube-system
  labels:
    app: cluster-autoscaler
spec:
  replicas: 1
  selector:
    matchLabels:
      app: cluster-autoscaler
  template:
    metadata:
      labels:
        app: cluster-autoscaler
    spec:
      serviceAccountName: cluster-autoscaler
      containers:
        - name: cluster-autoscaler
          image: registry.k8s.io/autoscaling/cluster-autoscaler:v1.28.0
          command:
            - ./cluster-autoscaler
            - --v=4
            - --stderrthreshold=info
            - --cloud-provider=aws
            - --skip-nodes-with-local-storage=false
```

```
      - --scale-down-enabled=true
      - --balance-similar-node-groups
    resources:
      limits:
        cpu: 100m
        memory: 300Mi
      requests:
        cpu: 100m
        memory: 300Mi
    volumeMounts:
      - mountPath: /etc/kubernetes/pki
        name: ssl-certs
        readOnly: true
  volumes:
    - name: ssl-certs
      hostPath:
        path: /etc/kubernetes/pki
```

**3. Configuring Auto-Scaling**

**AWS EKS: Configuring Node Groups**

In AWS EKS, auto-scaling requires defining a **Managed Node Group**. You set **minimum, maximum, and desired instance counts**:

```
aws eks create-nodegroup \
  --cluster-name my-cluster \
  --nodegroup-name my-node-group \
  --scaling-config minSize=1,maxSize=5,desiredSize=2 \
  --subnets subnet-abc123 subnet-def456 \
  --instance-types t3.medium
```

**GKE: Configuring Node Pools**

For Google Kubernetes Engine (GKE), you define an auto-scaling node pool:

```
gcloud container node-pools create my-node-pool \
  --cluster my-cluster \
  --num-nodes 1 \
  --enable-autoscaling \
  --min-nodes 1 \
  --max-nodes 5 \
  --machine-type n1-standard-2
```

**4. Verifying Cluster Autoscaler**

**Check Logs**

kubectl logs -f deployment/cluster-autoscaler -n kube-system

**Check Node Scaling**

- List nodes in the cluster:
  kubectl get nodes
- List unscheduled Pods:
  kubectl get pods --all-namespaces | grep Pending
- Describe an unscheduled Pod to find scheduling failures:
  kubectl describe pod <pod-name>

**5. Tuning Cluster Autoscaler**

You can fine-tune CA with different flags:

| Flag | Description |
|---|---|
| --scale-down-enabled=true | Enables scale-down of underutilized nodes |
| --skip-nodes-with-local-storage=false | Allows nodes with local storage to be scaled down |
| --balance-similar-node-groups | Balances workloads across node groups |
| --expander=least-waste | Prioritizes least-waste node selection for scaling |

**Conclusion**

Cluster Autoscaler is essential for cost-effective and efficient Kubernetes cluster management. It dynamically adds nodes when workloads increase and removes them when they're underutilized. Proper configuration ensures optimal performance and cost savings.

# Resource Requests and Limits in Kubernetes

In Kubernetes, **Resource Requests and Limits** are used to manage CPU and memory allocation for containers within a Pod. These settings help optimize cluster resources, prevent resource starvation, and ensure fair scheduling.

## 1. Understanding Resource Requests and Limits

### 1.1 Resource Requests

- Specifies the **minimum** amount of CPU and memory that a container requires.
- The Kubernetes scheduler **uses these values** to decide on which node to place the Pod.
- If a node has insufficient resources, the Pod remains in a Pending state.

### 1.2 Resource Limits

- Defines the **maximum** amount of CPU and memory a container can use.
- If a container exceeds the CPU limit, it is **throttled** (slowed down).
- If a container exceeds the memory limit, Kubernetes **kills** the container (OOMKill).

## 2. Defining Resource Requests and Limits in a Pod

You define resource requests and limits inside the Pod's YAML file under the resources field.

**Example: Pod with Resource Requests and Limits**

```
apiVersion: v1
kind: Pod
metadata:
  name: resource-demo
spec:
  containers:
    - name: my-container
      image: nginx
```

```
resources:
  requests:
    memory: "64Mi"   # Minimum 64MB memory required
    cpu: "250m"      # Minimum 0.25 CPU required
  limits:
    memory: "128Mi"  # Max 128MB memory allowed
    cpu: "500m"      # Max 0.5 CPU allowed
```

**Explanation**

- The container **requests**:
  - 64Mi (64MB) of memory
  - 250m (0.25 CPU core)
- The container **limits**:
  - 128Mi (128MB) of memory
  - 500m (0.5 CPU core)
- Kubernetes **guarantees at least 64MB of memory and 0.25 CPU** but does not allow the container to exceed 128MB of memory or 0.5 CPU.

**3. How CPU and Memory Work in Kubernetes**

**3.1 CPU Requests & Limits**

- **Measured in millicores (m)**:
  - 1000m = 1 CPU core
  - 500m = 0.5 CPU core
- **Behavior**:
  - If a container exceeds its CPU **request**, it may still use more CPU **if available**.
  - If a container exceeds its CPU **limit**, Kubernetes throttles (slows down) the container.

**3.2 Memory Requests & Limits**

- **Measured in bytes (Mi for Mebibytes, Gi for Gibibytes)**.
- **Behaviour**:
  - If a container exceeds its memory **request**, it may still use more if available.
  - If a container exceeds its memory **limit**, Kubernetes **kills it (OOMKilled)**.

**4. Verifying Resource Allocation**

Once you create a Pod, you can check its resource allocation.

### 4.1 Get Pod Details

kubectl describe pod resource-demo

**Output (Example)**

```
Name:         resource-demo
Namespace:    default
Containers:
  my-container:
    CPU Requests:  250m
    CPU Limits:    500m
    Memory Requests:  64Mi
    Memory Limits:    128Mi
```

### 4.2 Monitor Resource Usage

To check real-time resource usage, use:

kubectl top pod resource-demo

### 5. Setting Requests and Limits at Namespace Level Using a ResourceQuota

A **ResourceQuota** restricts the total resource usage for a namespace.

```
apiVersion: v1
kind: ResourceQuota
metadata:
  name: namespace-quota
  namespace: my-namespace
spec:
  hard:
    requests.cpu: "1"       # Total CPU requests across all Pods
cannot exceed 1 core
    requests.memory: "512Mi"
    limits.cpu: "2"
    limits.memory: "1Gi"
```

- This ensures all Pods within the namespace **share resources within limits**.

### 6. Setting Default Requests & Limits with LimitRange

A **LimitRange** sets default requests and limits for Pods in a namespace.

```
apiVersion: v1
kind: LimitRange
metadata:
  name: default-limits
  namespace: my-namespace
spec:
  limits:
    - default:
        memory: "256Mi"
        cpu: "500m"
      defaultRequest:
        memory: "128Mi"
        cpu: "250m"
      type: Container
```

- If a Pod **does not define** requests/limits, Kubernetes applies these defaults.

**7. Common Issues and Troubleshooting**

**7.1 Pod Stuck in "Pending"**

```
kubectl get pods
kubectl describe pod <pod-name>
```

**Possible Reasons:**

- The node **does not have enough free resources** to satisfy the request.
- Check available resources using:
  kubectl top nodes

- ## 7.2 Container Gets OOMKilled

  ```
  kubectl describe pod <pod-name>
  ```

If you see:
makefile
CopyEdit
State:    Terminated
Reason:    OOMKilled

**Solution:** Increase the memory limit.

### 7.3 CPU Throttling

- If your application runs slower than expected, check throttling using:

  kubectl logs <pod-name>
- Increase the CPU limit if needed.

## 8. Best Practices

✓ **Always set resource requests and limits** to prevent over-provisioning.
✓ **Monitor CPU and memory usage** using kubectl top pod.
✓ **Use ResourceQuota** to prevent excessive resource consumption in a namespace.
✓ **Set default requests and limits** using **LimitRange**.
✓ **Test with realistic values** before setting strict limits to avoid performance issues.

## Conclusion

Resource Requests and Limits in Kubernetes help **efficiently manage resources**, prevent **overloading nodes**, and ensure **fair resource allocation**. Properly configuring them **improves cluster stability** and **cost optimization**.

# Part-2

# Advanced Kubernetes Topics

# Custom Resource Definitions (CRDs) and Operators

## What are CRDs and Operators in Kubernetes?

**1. Custom Resource Definitions (CRDs)**

CRDs let you **extend the Kubernetes API**. You can define your own resource types (like MySQLCluster, Cache, etc.) just like native ones (Pod, Deployment, etc.).

**Use Case**: Suppose you want to manage Redis clusters as a first-class citizen in Kubernetes. You can create a RedisCluster CRD, and then interact with kubectl like this:

```
kubectl get redisclusters
kubectl apply -f my-redis-cluster.yaml
```

**2. Operators**

An **Operator** is a **controller** that watches custom resources and performs actions to reconcile their desired state with reality.

**Analogy**: Think of CRDs as the *"what"* (resource structure), and Operators as the *"how"* (logic for managing the resource).

**Example: Create a CRD and Write an Operator**

**Step 1: Define a CRD**

We'll create a simple CRD for a CronTab (like a cron job manager).

```yaml
# crd.yaml
apiVersion: apiextensions.k8s.io/v1
kind: CustomResourceDefinition
metadata:
  name: crontabs.stable.example.com
spec:
  group: stable.example.com
  names:
    kind: CronTab
    listKind: CronTabList
    plural: crontabs
    singular: crontab
  scope: Namespaced
  versions:
    - name: v1
      served: true
      storage: true
      schema:
        openAPIV3Schema:
          type: object
          properties:
            spec:
              type: object
              properties:
                schedule:
                  type: string
                image:
                  type: string
```

Apply it:

```
kubectl apply -f crd.yaml
```

**Step 2: Create a Custom Resource**

```yaml
# crontab.yaml
apiVersion: stable.example.com/v1
kind: CronTab
metadata:
  name: my-cron
spec:
  schedule: "* * * * *"
  image: busybox
```

Apply it:

```
kubectl apply -f crontab.yaml
```

**Step 3: Write a Simple Operator (Python Client Example)**
Here's a minimal Operator using the kubernetes Python client.

```
# operator.py
from kubernetes import client, config, watch

def main():
  config.load_kube_config()  # or load_incluster_config() if
running in cluster
  api = client.CustomObjectsApi()
  w = watch.Watch()

  for event in w.stream(api.list_namespaced_custom_object,
                group="stable.example.com",
                version="v1",
                namespace="default",
                plural="crontabs"):
    crontab = event['object']
    event_type = event['type']
    name = crontab['metadata']['name']
    spec = crontab['spec']

    print(f"Event: {event_type} - CronTab: {name}")
    print(f"  Schedule: {spec['schedule']}")
    print(f"  Image: {spec['image']}")

    # Here you can implement logic to create Kubernetes
Jobs based on the schedule

if __name__ == "__main__":
  main()
```

Run it locally (or package it into a container and deploy as a Pod).

**Optional: Use Operator SDK (Go-based)**

If you're using Go, operator-sdk scaffolds everything for you.

```
operator-sdk init --domain example.com --repo
github.com/example/my-operator
operator-sdk create api --group stable --version v1 --kind
CronTab --resource –controller
```

It gives you:

- CRD definition
- Controller logic
- Reconciliation loop
- Test scaffolding

**Summary**

| Component | Purpose |
|---|---|
| **CRD** | Defines your own resource types |
| **Operator** | Watches those resources and acts on them |
| **Controller** | Core part of the Operator that does the reconciliation |
| **kubectl + YAML** | You interact with your CRDs like native resources |

# Extending Kubernetes with CRDs

Kubernetes comes with a set of built-in resource types like:

- Pods
- Services
- Deployments

But you can **create your own types** by using **Custom Resource Definitions (CRDs)**. This lets you add *custom APIs* to Kubernetes—without modifying the core codebase.

**Why Do This?**

Because you might want to manage:

- A database cluster (PostgresCluster)
- A job runner (DataPipeline)
- An internal business service (FeatureFlag, Tenant, etc.)

**CRDs in Action: Step-by-Step Example**

**Step 1: Define a CRD**

Here's a YAML file to create a CronTab resource (a scheduled job spec).

```yaml
# crd.yaml
apiVersion: apiextensions.k8s.io/v1
kind: CustomResourceDefinition
metadata:
  name: crontabs.stable.example.com
spec:
  group: stable.example.com
  names:
    plural: crontabs
    singular: crontab
    kind: CronTab
    shortNames:
      - ct
  scope: Namespaced
  versions:
    - name: v1
      served: true
      storage: true
      schema:
        openAPIV3Schema:
          type: object
          properties:
            spec:
              type: object
              properties:
                schedule:
                  type: string
                image:
                  type: string
```

**Apply it:**

```
kubectl apply -f crd.yaml
```

Now you've added a *new Kubernetes object type*: CronTab.

**Step 2: Use Your Custom Resource**

Now define a new instance of your CronTab type:

```yaml
# crontab-example.yaml
apiVersion: stable.example.com/v1
```

```
kind: CronTab
metadata:
  name: backup-job
spec:
  schedule: "0 2 * * *"
  image: busybox
```

**Apply it:**

kubectl apply -f crontab-example.yaml

Now kubectl get crontabs works:

kubectl get crontabs

**Step 3: Add Behavior with a Controller (Optional)**
You can write a controller that watches CronTab resources and acts on them. That's where **Operators** come in (covered earlier). This is optional—but it makes your CRDs *do* things, like create Pods or Jobs.

**Recap: How CRDs Extend Kubernetes**

| **Feature** | **Built-in Resources** | **Custom Resources** |
|---|---|---|
| Type | Pod, Service, etc. | MyApp, CronTab, etc. |
| Defined by | Kubernetes core | You (via CRD) |
| Managed by | Built-in controllers | Your controller/operator |
| Accessed via | kubectl | Same (kubectl get myapps) |

**When to Use CRDs**

Use CRDs when:

- You want to **create reusable abstractions** (e.g., DatabaseBackup, AppCluster)
- You need to **codify business logic** into the Kubernetes model
- You're building **a platform on top of Kubernetes**

# Writing and Deploying Operators

**What Is an Operator?**

An **Operator** automates the management of a Kubernetes resource—especially a **Custom Resource** you've defined with a CRD.

Think of it like this:

CRD = *"What you want to manage".*
Operator = *"How it gets managed."*
You can write Operators in Go, Python, or even bash (using tools like **Operator SDK**, **kopf**, or **Kubebuilder**).

**Option 1: Writing an Operator in Python using kopf**

Let's build a simple Operator that manages our earlier CronTab resource using kopf.

**Step 1: Install kopf**

pip install kopf Kubernetes

**Step 2: Operator Code (Python)**

```
# crontab_operator.py
import kopf
import kubernetes

@kopf.on.create('stable.example.com', 'v1', 'crontabs')
def create_fn(spec, name, namespace, **kwargs):
   schedule = spec.get('schedule')
   image = spec.get('image')

   print(f"Creating CronTab '{name}' with schedule '{schedule}'
and image '{image}'")

   # Create a job or deployment based on this
   api = kubernetes.client.CoreV1Api()
   pod_manifest = {
      'apiVersion': 'v1',
```

```
        'kind': 'Pod',
        'metadata': {'name': f'{name}-pod'},
        'spec': {
            'containers': [{
                'name': 'job',
                'image': image,
                'args': ['echo', f"Running {name}"],
            }],
            'restartPolicy': 'OnFailure'
        }
    }
    api.create_namespaced_pod(namespace=namespace,
body=pod_manifest)
```

**Step 3: Run Operator (Locally)**

You can test this by running it outside the cluster:

```
kopf run crontab_operator.py
```

Just make sure you've already applied:

- The CRD
- A sample CronTab object

**Step 4: Deploy Operator to Cluster**

To deploy this as a Kubernetes Pod:

**1. Dockerfile**

```
FROM python:3.10-slim
RUN pip install kopf kubernetes
COPY crontab_operator.py /app/
WORKDIR /app
CMD ["kopf", "run", "--standalone", "crontab_operator.py"]
```

**2. Build and Push**

```
docker build -t yourname/crontab-operator .
docker push yourname/crontab-operator
```

**3. Deploy as Kubernetes Pod**

```
# operator-deployment.yaml
apiVersion: apps/v1
```

```
kind: Deployment
metadata:
  name: crontab-operator
spec:
  replicas: 1
  selector:
    matchLabels:
      app: crontab-operator
  template:
    metadata:
      labels:
        app: crontab-operator
    spec:
      serviceAccountName: default  # Use a proper one with
RBAC in production
      containers:
      - name: operator
        image: yourname/crontab-operator
```

Apply it:

```
kubectl apply -f operator-deployment.yaml
```

Now your Operator runs *inside the cluster* and watches CronTab resources.

**Add RBAC (Recommended)**

Operators need permissions to read/write CRDs and other resources.

```
# rbac.yaml
apiVersion: rbac.authorization.k8s.io/v1
kind: Role
metadata:
  name: crontab-operator
rules:
- apiGroups: ["", "stable.example.com"]
  resources: ["pods", "crontabs"]
  verbs: ["get", "watch", "list", "create"]

---
apiVersion: rbac.authorization.k8s.io/v1
kind: RoleBinding
metadata:
  name: crontab-operator-binding
subjects:
- kind: ServiceAccount
```

```
  name: default
roleRef:
  kind: Role
  name: crontab-operator
  apiGroup: rbac.authorization.k8s.io
```

Apply:

```
kubectl apply -f rbac.yaml
```

**Option 2: Writing an Operator in Go using operator-sdk**

If you're doing enterprise-level automation, the Operator SDK (Go) is the industry standard.

```
operator-sdk init --domain example.com --repo github.com/example/crontab-operator
operator-sdk create api --group stable --version v1 --kind CronTab --resource –controller
```

It scaffolds everything:

- CRD
- Controller logic
- Reconciler loop
- RBAC, testing, and Dockerization

But it's heavier and Go-specific.

**Summary**

| Step | Action |
|---|---|
| 1 | Define a CRD |
| 2 | Write Operator logic (Python, Go, etc.) |
| 3 | Run locally for dev/test |
| 4 | Dockerize and deploy in-cluster |
| 5 | Apply RBAC so it can operate safely |

# Service Mesh and Traffic Management

**What is a Service Mesh?**

A **Service Mesh** is a dedicated infrastructure layer that handles **service-to-service communication** in a **secure, observable, and controlled** way.

**Core Capabilities:**

- **Traffic management** (routing, retries, timeouts)
- **Security** (mTLS, policy enforcement)
- **Observability** (metrics, tracing, logs)
- **Resilience** (circuit breakers, failovers)

**Popular Service Meshes**

| Tool | Language | Highlights |
|---|---|---|
| **Istio** | Envoy-based | Feature-rich, complex, enterprise-grade |
| **Linkerd** | Rust + Go | Lightweight, easy to use, minimal config |
| **Consul** | Go | Works across Kubernetes + VMs, strong integration with HashiCorp stack |

**Use Case: Canary Deployments & Traffic Splitting**

**1. ISTIO – Full-Featured Powerhouse**

**Setup (Quick Summary)**

Install via istioctl:

```
istioctl install --set profile=demo -y
kubectl label namespace default istio-injection=enabled
```

**Traffic Management with Istio**

**1.1 Define VirtualService and DestinationRule for traffic routing:**

```yaml
# destination-rule.yaml
apiVersion: networking.istio.io/v1beta1
kind: DestinationRule
metadata:
  name: reviews-dest
spec:
  host: reviews
  subsets:
  - name: v1
    labels:
      version: v1
  - name: v2
    labels:
      version: v2

# virtual-service.yaml
apiVersion: networking.istio.io/v1beta1
kind: VirtualService
metadata:
  name: reviews-route
spec:
  hosts:
  - reviews
  http:
  - route:
    - destination:
        host: reviews
        subset: v1
      weight: 80
    - destination:
        host: reviews
        subset: v2
      weight: 20
```

This sends **80%** of traffic to v1, **20%** to v2.

**2. LINKERD – Lightweight and Easy**

**Setup**

```
curl -sL https://run.linkerd.io/install | sh
linkerd install | kubectl apply -f -
```

```
linkerd check
```

Inject proxy into your namespace or specific deployments:

```
kubectl annotate ns default linkerd.io/inject=enabled
```

**Traffic Splitting with Linkerd**

You need to install the **linkerd-smi** extension:

```
linkerd install --crds | kubectl apply -f -
linkerd viz install | kubectl apply -f -
linkerd smi install | kubectl apply -f –
```

Use **SMI TrafficSplit** CRD:

```
# trafficsplit.yaml
apiVersion: split.smi-spec.io/v1alpha2
kind: TrafficSplit
metadata:
  name: reviews-split
spec:
  service: reviews
  backends:
  - service: reviews-v1
    weight: 80
  - service: reviews-v2
    weight: 20
```

Same effect: 80/20 split between two versions of reviews.

**3. CONSUL – Flexible and Cross-Platform**

**Setup**

Use Helm or CLI:

```
helm repo add hashicorp https://helm.releases.hashicorp.com
helm install consul hashicorp/consul --set global.name=consul
```

Enable Connect (Consul's service mesh feature), then inject sidecars.

**Traffic Management with Consul**

Consul uses **Intentions** + **Service Resolvers** to define routing logic.

Example: Split traffic with **ServiceRouter** and **ServiceSplitter**.

```
# service-splitter.yaml
apiVersion: consul.hashicorp.com/v1alpha1
kind: ServiceSplitter
metadata:
  name: reviews
spec:
  splits:
    - weight: 80
      serviceSubset: v1
    - weight: 20
      serviceSubset: v2

# service-router.yaml
apiVersion: consul.hashicorp.com/v1alpha1
kind: ServiceRouter
metadata:
  name: reviews
spec:
  routes:
    - match:
        http:
          pathPrefix: /
      destination:
        service: reviews
```

Just like in Istio/Linkerd, this gives you fine-grained traffic control.

**Security: All 3 Support mTLS**

| Feature | Istio | Linkerd | Consul |
|---|---|---|---|
| mTLS | ✅ | ✅ (auto) | ✅ |
| Authorization policies | ✅ | Limited | ✅ |
| Multi-cluster | ✅ | ✅ (manual) | ✅ (built-in) |

**Observability: All 3 Offer Built-in Telemetry**

- **Istio**: Grafana + Prometheus + Kiali

- **Linkerd**: linkerd viz – simple dashboard
- **Consul**: Integrates with Grafana + Datadog

**Summary: Which One Should You Use?**

| **You want...** | **Use** |
|---|---|
| Enterprise-grade features | **Istio** |
| Lightweight and minimal config | **Linkerd** |
| Integration with HashiCorp tools or hybrid infra | **Consul** |

# Service Mesh, Traffic Management & Sidecar Pattern in Kubernetes

These three concepts go hand-in-hand. Let's tackle them together to understand **how modern Kubernetes networking works**, especially in microservices environments.

**1. What Is Traffic Management in Kubernetes?**

Kubernetes by default offers basic traffic handling via:

- **ClusterIP / NodePort / LoadBalancer Services**
- **Ingress Controllers**

But it lacks:

- Fine-grained routing (e.g. canary deployments)
- Resiliency features (e.g. retries, timeouts)
- Observability of internal traffic

That's where **Service Mesh** comes in.

**2. What Is a Service Mesh?**

A **Service Mesh** is a dedicated infrastructure layer that controls **how services communicate**.

**It adds features like:**

- 🚦 **Advanced traffic routing** (canary, blue-green, A/B testing)
- 🔐 **Security** (mTLS between services)
- 📊 **Observability** (metrics, tracing)
- 💥 **Resilience** (circuit breaking, retries, failover)

Popular service meshes:

- **Istio** (feature-rich)
- **Linkerd** (lightweight, easy)
- **Consul** (hybrid, HashiCorp ecosystem)

**3. What's a Sidecar Pattern?**

The **Sidecar Pattern** is the **mechanism** used by service meshes.

**Sidecar = a helper container running alongside your app in the same Pod.**

This helper:

- Intercepts and manages all traffic (like a proxy)
- Runs independently from your app code
- Is often an **Envoy proxy** or similar lightweight proxy

**Example: How Service Mesh Uses Sidecars**

When using **Istio** or **Linkerd**, each of your service Pods will have:

- Your app container
- An injected **sidecar proxy**

```
containers:
- name: my-app
  image: my-app:latest
- name: istio-proxy
  image: istio/proxyv2
```

The proxy (sidecar):

- Handles **all ingress/egress traffic**
- Implements traffic routing, retries, load balancing, encryption

You talk to http://serviceA, but actually:

CSS:

[my-app] --> [sidecar proxy] --> [network] --> [sidecar proxy] --> [serviceB]

You never talk directly — the **sidecars control the flow**.

**4. Traffic Management via Service Mesh**

Here's how **Istio** handles traffic control:

**Route 90% of traffic to v1, 10% to v2:**

```
apiVersion: networking.istio.io/v1beta1
kind: VirtualService
metadata:
  name: my-app
spec:
  hosts:
  - my-app
  http:
  - route:
    - destination:
        host: my-app
        subset: v1
      weight: 90
    - destination:
        host: my-app
        subset: v2
      weight: 10
```

This works because the **sidecars implement this logic**, as defined by the mesh controller.

**Traffic Management Examples by Tool**

| Feature | Istio | Linkerd | Consul |
|---|---|---|---|
| Traffic Splitting | ✅ (VirtualService) | ✅ (SMI TrafficSplit) | ✅ (ServiceSplitter) |
| Retries/Timeouts | ✅ | ✅ | ✅ |
| Canary Deployments | ✅ | ✅ | ✅ |
| Observability | Grafana, Kiali, Prometheus | Built-in dashboard | Integrates with Datadog/Grafana |

**Summary**

| Concept | Description |
|---|---|
| **Service Mesh** | Infrastructure layer managing service-to-service communication |
| **Traffic Management** | Features like routing, retries, circuit-breaking |
| **Sidecar Pattern** | A design pattern where a helper container (proxy) runs alongside the app to intercept traffic |
| **Why it matters** | You get secure, observable, and resilient communication **without changing your app code** |

# Multi-Cluster and Hybrid Deployments

**Why Multi-Cluster?**

As your infrastructure grows, you might need:

- High availability across regions
- Regulatory/geographic boundaries (e.g. data locality)
- Disaster recovery
- Migration (e.g. on-prem → cloud)
- Isolation between teams or environments

This is where **multi-cluster** and **hybrid deployments** come in.

**Common Approaches to Multi-Cluster**

| Method | Description |
|---|---|
| **Federation** | Centralized control plane syncs resources to clusters |
| **Service Mesh (e.g., Istio multi-cluster)** | Mesh handles service discovery and traffic |
| **Custom Controllers / CI pipelines** | Push workloads selectively via automation |

| Method | Description |
|---|---|
| **Cluster API / GitOps** | Treat clusters as deployable units (GitOps manages them) |

# Part 1: Federation

**What is Kubernetes Federation?**

**Kubernetes Federation** lets you **sync resources (like Deployments, Services, etc.) across clusters** using a **central control plane**.

Key idea: Define once → deploy to multiple clusters.

**Setup: KubeFed (Kubernetes Federation v2)**

Install KubeFed using Helm:

```
helm repo add kubefed-charts https://raw.githubusercontent.com/kubernetes-sigs/kubefed/master/charts
helm install kubefed kubefed-charts/kubefed --namespace kube-federation-system --create-namespace
```

Join clusters:

```
kubefedctl join cluster1 --host-cluster-context=cluster1 --add-to-registry --v=2
kubefedctl join cluster2 --host-cluster-context=cluster1 --add-to-registry --v=2
```

**Example: Federated Deployment**

```
apiVersion: types.kubefed.io/v1beta1
kind: FederatedDeployment
metadata:
  name: nginx
  namespace: default
spec:
  template:
    metadata:
      labels:
```

```yaml
    app: nginx
spec:
  replicas: 2
  selector:
    matchLabels:
      app: nginx
  template:
    metadata:
      labels:
        app: nginx
    spec:
      containers:
      - name: nginx
        image: nginx:latest
        ports:
        - containerPort: 80
```

This will deploy the same nginx Deployment in all **joined clusters**.

**Advanced: Per-cluster overrides**

```yaml
spec:
  overrides:
  - clusterName: cluster1
    clusterOverrides:
    - path: "/spec/replicas"
      value: 3
  - clusterName: cluster2
    clusterOverrides:
    - path: "/spec/replicas"
      value: 1
```

# Part 2: Managing Multi-Cluster Workloads (Without Federation)

**Strategy: Use Labels, Selective CI/CD, or GitOps**

A more flexible (and often preferred) way is to treat each cluster as an independent environment and **deploy to them selectively**.

**Option 1: GitOps (e.g. ArgoCD, Flux)**

You maintain **one Git repo**, and apply **cluster-specific overlays** using Kustomize or Helm.

Example file tree:

```
deployments/
├── base/
│   └── deployment.yaml
├── overlays/
│   ├── cluster1/
│   │   └── kustomization.yaml
│   └── cluster2/
│       └── kustomization.yaml
```

You apply these via ArgoCD apps or Flux Kustomizations:

```
# cluster1 app
apiVersion: argoproj.io/v1alpha1
kind: Application
metadata:
  name: nginx-cluster1
spec:
  destination:
    server: https://<cluster1-api>
    namespace: default
  source:
    path: deployments/overlays/cluster1
```

This way, you can:

- Customize resources per cluster
- Roll out selectively
- Use Git as the source of truth

**Option 2: Multi-Cluster Service Mesh (e.g., Istio)**

Istio lets services in one cluster **talk to services in another** (mesh-connected).

- Istio control planes share root trust
- Sidecars route traffic across clusters using ServiceEntry

```
apiVersion: networking.istio.io/v1beta1
kind: ServiceEntry
metadata:
  name: ratings-remote
```

```
spec:
  hosts:
  - ratings.default.global
  location: MESH_INTERNAL
  ports:
  - number: 9080
    name: http
    protocol: HTTP
  resolution: DNS
  addresses:
  - 240.0.0.1
  endpoints:
  - address: 10.20.30.40  # Cluster2 IP
```

**Hybrid Deployments: On-Prem + Cloud**

When mixing **cloud clusters and on-prem**, you can use:

- VPNs to connect networks
- External DNS or service mesh for discovery
- Shared GitOps + secrets tooling (like Vault)

Example use cases:

- Cloud for burst capacity
- On-prem for sensitive data
- Active/standby disaster recovery

**Tools to Manage Multi-Cluster**

| Tool | Use |
|---|---|
| **KubeFed** | Declarative multi-cluster sync |
| **Istio / Linkerd** | Cross-cluster service discovery + mTLS |
| **ArgoCD / Flux** | GitOps-based deployment |
| **Rancher** | GUI for managing many clusters |
| **Cluster API** | Provisioning + lifecycle management of clusters |

**Summary**

| Topic | What You Do |
|---|---|
| **Federation** | Define one resource, sync to many clusters |

| **Topic** | **What You Do** |
|---|---|
| **Multi-Cluster GitOps** | Define per-cluster configs, manage via ArgoCD/Flux |
| **Service Mesh** | Connect services securely across clusters |
| **Hybrid Deployments** | Combine on-prem + cloud, with network/service stitching |

# Part 3:

# Running Kubernetes in Production

# CI/CD with Kubernetes

## 1. What Is CI/CD in Kubernetes?

**CI/CD** = Continuous Integration + Continuous Deployment.
In Kubernetes, CI/CD means:

- **CI**: Build/test your code → create container images.
- **CD**: Deploy to a cluster automatically using Git or a pipeline.

Modern CD focuses on **GitOps**.

## 2. GitOps: ArgoCD vs Flux

**GitOps** is the idea of using **Git as the source of truth** for your deployments.

- Kubernetes manifests live in Git
- Tools **watch Git** and sync changes to the cluster
- Changes are **tracked, reviewed, auditable**

**ArgoCD and Flux both:**

- Sync cluster state from Git
- Detect and auto-apply changes
- Support Helm, Kustomize, raw YAML
- Provide rollback/versioning via Git

### ArgoCD: GitOps with a UI

**Install ArgoCD**

```
kubectl create namespace argocd
kubectl apply -n argocd -f https://raw.githubusercontent.com/argoproj/argo-cd/stable/manifests/install.yaml
```

**Access UI**

```
kubectl port-forward svc/argocd-server -n argocd 8080:443
```

Log in with:

```
kubectl get secret argocd-initial-admin-secret -n argocd -o jsonpath="{.data.password}" | base64 -d
```

**Define an Application**

```
# argo-app.yaml
apiVersion: argoproj.io/v1alpha1
kind: Application
metadata:
  name: my-app
  namespace: argocd
spec:
  destination:
    server: https://kubernetes.default.svc
    namespace: default
  source:
    repoURL: https://github.com/your-org/your-repo
    targetRevision: main
    path: k8s/overlays/prod
  project: default
  syncPolicy:
    automated:
      prune: true
      selfHeal: true
```

Apply:

```
kubectl apply -f argo-app.yaml
```

ArgoCD will now **watch your Git repo** and deploy anything under that path.

**Flux: Lightweight GitOps via Controllers**

**Install Flux**

```
curl -s https://fluxcd.io/install.sh | sudo bash
flux install
```

**Bootstrap with Git**

```
flux bootstrap github \
  --owner=my-org \
```

```
  --repository=my-repo \
  --branch=main \
  --path=clusters/my-cluster
```

Flux will:

- Push manifests to your repo
- Watch them
- Sync them to the cluster

### 3. Helm for Kubernetes Packaging

**Helm** is like a package manager for Kubernetes.

#### Helm Chart Structure

Bash:

```
helm create my-app
```

YAML:

```
# values.yaml
replicaCount: 2
image:
  repository: nginx
  tag: latest
```

Bash:

```
helm install my-app ./my-app-chart
```

Or upgrade:

Bash:

```
helm upgrade my-app ./my-app-chart --values=values-prod.yaml
```

Helm + ArgoCD: ArgoCD can track Helm charts in Git:

YAML:

```
source:
  repoURL: https://github.com/my-org/my-helm-repo
  path: charts/my-app
  helm:
    valueFiles:
    - values.yaml
```

### 4. Kustomize for Declarative Patching

**Kustomize** lets you maintain:

- Base templates
- Overlays for dev, staging, prod

**Structure:**

```
k8s/
├── base/
│   ├── deployment.yaml
│   └── kustomization.yaml
├── overlays/
│   ├── dev/
│   └── prod/
```

**Example kustomization.yaml**

```
resources:
  - ../../base
patchesStrategicMerge:
  - deployment-patch.yaml
```

Run locally:

kustomize build overlays/prod | kubectl apply -f –

Use in ArgoCD or Flux as the Git path.

**CI/CD Flow (End-to-End)**

1. **Push code to Git**
2. CI (GitHub Actions, GitLab, Jenkins) builds + pushes image
3. CI updates the manifest in Git (with new image tag)
4. GitOps tool (ArgoCD/Flux) sees the Git change
5. It **syncs to cluster** → New version deployed

**Summary**

| Tool | Purpose |
|---|---|
| **ArgoCD** | GitOps tool with GUI and automation |
| **Flux** | Lightweight GitOps with GitHub/GitLab native workflows |

| Tool | Purpose |
|---|---|
| **Helm** | Package and template Kubernetes resources |
| **Kustomize** | Overlay-specific customizations |

# Disaster Recovery and Backup

Disasters in Kubernetes can come from:

- Node or cluster failure
- Accidental deletion of resources
- Data loss (e.g., from PersistentVolumes)
- Corrupted or failed control plane (including etcd)

Your job is to ensure you can **recover quickly and reliably**.

### 1. Backup Strategies for Kubernetes

You need to back up:

1. **Cluster state** (control plane, especially etcd)
2. **Application resources** (Deployments, Services, etc.)
3. **Persistent data** (PVCs, volumes, DBs)

### General Backup Strategies

| Type | Tool/Approach | What It Protects |
|---|---|---|
| **Etcd snapshot** | Native etcdctl | Core Kubernetes config + cluster state |
| **YAML backups** | kubectl get all --export | Deployments, Services, CRDs |
| **Volume snapshots** | CSI snapshots or Velero | App data (e.g., DBs) |
| **Full solution** | Velero, Kasten, Stash | Cluster + volumes + apps |

### 2. etcd Snapshots & Restores

### What is etcd?

- etcd is a key-value store used by Kubernetes to store **everything about the cluster** (nodes, pods, config, secrets).
- It runs in the control plane.

**Backup etcd (Manual Snapshot)**

On the **control plane node** (assuming kubeadm), run:

```
ETCDCTL_API=3 etcdctl snapshot save /backup/etcd-snapshot.db \
  --endpoints=https://127.0.0.1:2379 \
  --cacert=/etc/kubernetes/pki/etcd/ca.crt \
  --cert=/etc/kubernetes/pki/etcd/server.crt \
  --key=/etc/kubernetes/pki/etcd/server.key
```

This saves a snapshot to /backup/etcd-snapshot.db.
Make sure to store this in a safe place (off-node, offsite ideally).

**Restore etcd Snapshot**

1. Stop kube-apiserver:

```
systemctl stop kubelet
docker stop etcd  # or crictl or containerd
```

2. Restore the snapshot:

```
ETCDCTL_API=3 etcdctl snapshot restore /backup/etcd-snapshot.db \
 --data-dir /var/lib/etcd-from-backup
```

3. Update etcd config (in kube manifest) to use the new data dir:

Edit /etc/kubernetes/manifests/etcd.yaml:

```
--data-dir=/var/lib/etcd-from-backup
```

4. Restart kubelet, which will re-launch etcd with the restored data.

**3. Full Backup Solutions**

**Velero (Most Popular Tool)**

Velero backs up:

- Namespaces
- Resources (Deployments, PVCs, etc.)
- Persistent volume data (if using supported plugins)

**Install Velero (example with AWS S3)**

```
velero install \
  --provider aws \
  --plugins velero/velero-plugin-for-aws:v1.5.0 \
  --bucket <YOUR-BUCKET> \
  --backup-location-config region=<REGION> \
  --secret-file ./credentials-velero
```

**Backup Example**

```
velero backup create my-backup --include-namespaces my-namespace
```

**Restore Example**

```
velero restore create --from-backup my-backup
```

You can schedule automated backups, too:

```
velero schedule create daily-backup --schedule="0 2 * * *"
```

**Tips for Real-World DR Readiness**

- ✅ Automate backups (etcd + volumes)
- ✅ Store off-cluster (S3, NFS, etc.)
- ✅ Test restores regularly
- ✅ Use labels and tags to filter critical resources
- ✅ Document restore procedures and time estimates

**Summary**

| Topic | Tool | Purpose |
|---|---|---|
| **Etcd backup** | etcdctl snapshot save | Save full cluster state |
| **Etcd restore** | etcdctl snapshot restore | Rebuild control plane |

| Topic | Tool | Purpose |
|---|---|---|
| **Cluster & app backup** | Velero, Kasten, Stash | Backup Kubernetes resources + volumes |
| **Best practice** | Automate, test, store offsite | DR readiness |

# Kubernetes on the Cloud

## 1. Kubernetes on Major Cloud Providers

All three cloud platforms offer **managed Kubernetes services**, so you don't have to manage the control plane yourself.

| Feature | EKS (AWS) | GKE (Google) | AKS (Azure) |
|---|---|---|---|
| Control Plane Cost | $0.10/hour (per cluster) | Free (Standard), Autopilot available | Free |
| Auto Scaling | ✅ Node groups, Karpenter | ✅ Node pools, Autopilot | ✅ VM scale sets |
| Upgrades | Manual/semi-auto | Auto or manual | Manual/semi-auto |
| Security | IAM, OIDC, KMS | IAM, workload identity | Azure AD, Key Vault |
| Network Model | VPC CNI | VPC-native | Azure CNI |
| Storage | EBS, EFS, FSx | PD, Filestore | Azure Disk/File |

**AWS EKS Highlights**

- **Provisioning**:

```
eksctl create cluster --name dev-cluster --region us-west-2 --nodes 2
```

- Supports **Fargate** for serverless pods
- Use **Karpenter** for smarter autoscaling and spot instance support

**Google GKE Highlights**

- **Autopilot mode**: Fully managed, pay-per-pod (great for small workloads)
- **Standard mode**: More control, pay-per-node

```
gcloud container clusters create my-cluster \
  --zone us-central1-a --num-nodes=2
```

- Native **integrations with Cloud Logging and Monitoring**

**Azure AKS Highlights**

- Easy RBAC integration with **Azure AD**
- **Node auto-upgrades and repair** built-in
- Works great with **Bicep** and **Terraform** for IaaS

```
az aks create --resource-group my-rg --name my-cluster --node-count 2 --enable-addons monitoring --generate-ssh-keys
```

# 2. Kubernetes Cost Optimization

Running Kubernetes in the cloud **can get expensive fast**. Here's how to keep it under control:

**General Cost-Saving Strategies**

| Area | Strategy |
|---|---|
| **Nodes** | Use **spot/preemptible VMs**, autoscaling |
| **Workloads** | Right-size CPU/memory, use resource quotas/limits |

| Area | Strategy |
|---|---|
| **Unused Resources** | Clean up orphaned PVCs, IPs, LoadBalancers |
| **Storage** | Use Delete reclaim policies, avoid premium storage if not needed |
| **Monitoring** | Offload logs/metrics to cheaper storage after a period |
| **Clusters** | Consolidate workloads, run fewer clusters when possible |

**Node Autoscaling Tools**

- **Karpenter (AWS)**: Launches optimal EC2 instances based on pod needs
- **GKE Autopilot**: Pay only for what you use (per pod)
- **Cluster Autoscaler**: Works with all clouds, scales nodes as needed

**Right-Sizing Resources**

Add **requests and limits** in your deployments:

```
resources:
  requests:
    cpu: "100m"
    memory: "128Mi"
  limits:
    cpu: "200m"
    memory: "256Mi"
```

Don't over-provision. Use tools like:

- **Goldilocks** (recommends optimal requests/limits)
- **Kubecost** (tracks resource cost and waste)

**Spot / Preemptible Instances**

| Provider | Spot Pricing Tool |
|---|---|
| AWS | EC2 Spot + Karpenter |
| GCP | Preemptible VMs |
| Azure | Spot VMs |

These can **cut costs by up to 90%**, great for:

- Batch jobs
- Non-critical workloads
- Auto-scalable deployments

**Example: Autoscaling on EKS with Karpenter**

Install Karpenter, then create a provisioner:

```
apiVersion: karpenter.sh/v1alpha5
kind: Provisioner
metadata:
  name: default
spec:
  requirements:
    - key: "instance-type"
      operator: In
      values: ["t3.medium", "m5.large"]
  limits:
    resources:
      cpu: 1000
  provider:
    subnetSelector:
      karpenter.sh/discovery: my-cluster
    securityGroupSelector:
      karpenter.sh/discovery: my-cluster
```

Now your cluster will automatically launch spot instances based on demand.

**Observability Tools for Cost and Performance**

| Tool | What It Does |
|---|---|
| **Kubecost** | Tracks real-time costs per namespace/deployment |
| **Goldilocks** | Recommends optimal CPU/memory values |
| **Grafana + Prometheus** | Monitor node/pod usage |
| **AWS Cost Explorer / GCP Billing** | Platform-level cost visibility |

**Summary**

| Topic | Key Points |
|---|---|
| **EKS** | Powerful, IAM-integrated, supports Karpenter & Fargate |
| **GKE** | Easy setup, Autopilot mode is cost-efficient |
| **AKS** | Azure-native, good AD integration |
| **Cost Optimization** | Spot instances, autoscaling, resource limits, cleanup |
| **Tools** | ArgoCD, Karpenter, Kubecost, Goldilocks, Velero |

# Appendices

## Common kubectl Commands

**What is kubectl?**

kubectl is the command-line tool for interacting with a Kubernetes cluster. It lets you manage and troubleshoot resources like pods, deployments, services, and more.

**1. Cluster Info & Configuration**

| Command | Description |
|---|---|
| kubectl version | Shows the client and server versions of Kubernetes. |
| kubectl config view | Displays kubeconfig settings. Useful to check contexts, clusters, and users. |
| kubectl config use-context CONTEXT_NAME | Switches to a different cluster context. |
| kubectl cluster-info | Displays basic info about the cluster's API server and services. |
| kubectl get componentstatuses or kubectl get cs | Shows the status of core components like scheduler and controller-manager. |

**2. Working with Resources (Get, Create, Delete)**

**a. Get resources**

kubectl get pods # List pods in the current namespace

kubectl get pods -A # List pods across all namespaces

kubectl get svc # List services

kubectl get deployments # List deployments

kubectl get nodes # List cluster nodes

kubectl get all # List all resources in the namespace

**b. Create resources**

kubectl apply -f filename.yaml # Create or update resource from a YAML/JSON file

kubectl create deployment nginx --image=nginx # Create a deployment quickly

**c. Delete resources**

kubectl delete pod POD_NAME # Delete a specific pod

kubectl delete -f filename.yaml # Delete resources defined in the file

kubectl delete svc SERVICE_NAME # Delete a specific service

### 3. Inspect and Debug

| Command | Description |
|---|---|
| **kubectl describe pod POD_NAME** | **Detailed info on the pod including events and errors.** |
| **kubectl logs POD_NAME** | **View logs from a container in a pod.** |

| Command | Description |
|---|---|
| kubectl logs POD_NAME -c CONTAINER_NAME | If the pod has multiple containers, specify which one. |
| kubectl exec -it POD_NAME -- /bin/sh | Open a shell inside the container (interactive). |
| kubectl top pod | Show CPU/memory usage (requires Metrics Server). |
| kubectl events or kubectl get events | Show cluster events (helpful for debugging). |

**4. Updating Resources**

| Command | Description |
|---|---|
| kubectl edit deployment DEPLOYMENT_NAME | Opens the deployment in a text editor to modify it live. |
| kubectl scale deployment DEPLOYMENT_NAME --replicas=5 | Scales a deployment to 5 replicas. |
| kubectl rollout restart deployment DEPLOYMENT_NAME | Restarts the deployment (e.g., to trigger rolling update). |
| kubectl rollout status deployment DEPLOYMENT_NAME | Check the status of a deployment rollout. |
| kubectl patch | Update part of a resource using JSON or strategic merge patch. |

**5. Testing & Port Forwarding**

| Command | Description |
|---|---|
| kubectl run testpod --image=nginx --restart=Never | Run a one-off pod for testing. |

| Command | Description |
|---|---|
| kubectl port-forward pod/POD_NAME 8080:80 | Forward local port to pod. |
| kubectl port-forward svc/SERVICE_NAME 8080:80 | Forward port to a service. |
| kubectl proxy | Run a local proxy to the Kubernetes API server. |

**6. Namespaces**

| Command | Description |
|---|---|
| kubectl get namespaces | List all namespaces. |
| kubectl get pods -n NAMESPACE | List pods in a specific namespace. |
| kubectl create namespace NAME | Create a new namespace. |
| kubectl delete namespace NAME | Delete a namespace. |

**7. YAML Export & Dry Runs**

| Command | Description |
|---|---|
| kubectl get deployment nginx -o yaml | Output resource in YAML format. |
| kubectl apply -f file.yaml --dry-run=client | Simulate changes without applying them. |
| kubectl create deployment nginx --image=nginx --dry-run=client -o yaml | Generate YAML from CLI input. |

**8. Cleanups & Useful Shortcuts**

| Command | Description |
|---|---|
| kubectl delete pod --all | Delete all pods in the namespace. |

| Command | Description |
|---|---|
| kubectl get pods -o wide | Show more info (e.g., node, IPs). |
| kubectl get pods --watch | Continuously watch pod status changes. |
| kubectl get events --sort-by=.metadata.creationTimestamp | See latest events first. |

✅ Tips

- Use -n NAMESPACE to specify a namespace.
- Use --selector to filter by labels.
- Use -o json or -o yaml for programmatic output.
- Tab completion makes life easier (kubectl completion bash or zsh).

# YAML Configuration Examples

## 1. Pod

```
apiVersion: v1
kind: Pod
metadata:
  name: nginx-pod
spec:
  containers:
```

```
  - name: nginx-container
    image: nginx:latest
    ports:
      -containerPort:80
```

# 2. Deployment

```
apiVersion: apps/v1
kind: Deployment
metadata:
  name: nginx-deployment
spec:
  replicas: 3
  selector:
    matchLabels:
      app: nginx
  template:
    metadata:
      labels:
        app: nginx
    spec:
      containers:
        - name: nginx
          image: nginx:1.21
          ports:
            -containerPort:80
```

# 3. Service (ClusterIP)

```
apiVersion: v1
kind: Service
metadata:
  name: nginx-service
spec:
  selector:
    app: nginx
  ports:
    - protocol: TCP
      port: 80
```

```
    targetPort: 80
  type:ClusterIP
```

# 4. Service (NodePort)

```
apiVersion: v1
kind: Service
metadata:
  name: nginx-nodeport
spec:
  selector:
    app: nginx
  ports:
    - protocol: TCP
      port: 80
      targetPort: 80
      nodePort: 30007
  type:NodePort
```

# 5. ConfigMap

```
apiVersion: v1
kind: ConfigMap
metadata:
  name: app-config
data:
  APP_ENV: production
  LOG_LEVEL: info
```

# 6. Secret

```
apiVersion: v1
kind: Secret
metadata:
```

```
  name: db-secret
type: Opaque
data:
  username: YWRtaW4=        # base64 encoded 'admin'
  password: cGFzc3dvcmQ=    # base64 encoded 'password'
```

# 7. Ingress

```
apiVersion: networking.k8s.io/v1
kind: Ingress
metadata:
  name: example-ingress
  annotations:
    nginx.ingress.kubernetes.io/rewrite-target: /
spec:
  rules:
    - host: example.com
      http:
        paths:
          - path: /
            pathType: Prefix
            backend:
              service:
                name: nginx-service
                port:
                  number: 80
```

# 8. Namespace

```
apiVersion: v1
kind: Namespace
metadata:
  name: dev-environment
```

# 9. Job

```
apiVersion: batch/v1
kind: Job
metadata:
  name: hello-job
spec:
  template:
    spec:
      containers:
        - name: hello
          image: busybox
          command: ["echo", "Hello, Kubernetes"]
      restartPolicy: Never
  backoffLimit: 2
```

# 10. CronJob

```
apiVersion: batch/v1
kind: CronJob
metadata:
  name: hello-cron
spec:
  schedule: "*/5 * * * *"
  jobTemplate:
    spec:
      template:
        spec:
          containers:
            - name: hello
              image: busybox
              command: ["echo", "Hello from CronJob"]
          restartPolicy: OnFailure
```

# Troubleshooting Guide

Here's a **Kubernetes Troubleshooting Guide** that's clear, to the point, and focused on the most common problems you'll run into with kubectl and resources in the cluster.

## 1. General Troubleshooting Mindset

- Always **start with kubectl get** to confirm the resource exists.
- Use **kubectl describe** to check events and error messages.
- Check **logs**, especially for pods and containers.
- Use **kubectl get events --sort-by=.metadata.creationTimestamp** to see what failed recently.
- If all else fails, **check the node**, then go back up the chain (pod → deployment → node → cluster).

## 2. Pod Issues

### Pod Stuck in Pending

**Likely cause**: No resources (CPU/memory), or nodeSelector/taint issues.

kubectl describe pod <pod-name>

Look for:

- 0/3 nodes available (resource issue)
- nodeSelector, tolerations, affinity misconfiguration

**Fix**: Adjust scheduling rules or increase node capacity.

# Pod in CrashLoopBackOff or Error

**Likely cause**: Application crash, bad config, missing secrets, etc.

kubectl logs <pod-name> # For single-container pods
kubectl logs <pod-name> -c <container> # For multi-container pods

**Fix**:

- Check logs for stack traces or app errors.
- Validate configs or env vars via kubectl describe.
- Use kubectl exec -it <pod> -- /bin/sh to poke around inside.

# Pod in ImagePullBackOff or ErrImagePull

**Likely cause**: Image doesn't exist, wrong tag, or no registry access.

kubectl describe pod <pod-name>

Look for:

- Failed to pull image
- Unauthorized (private repo)

**Fix**:

- Check image name/tag.
- For private images, create a **secret** and reference it with imagePullSecrets.

# 3. Deployment Issues

## Deployment Not Updating

kubectl rollout status deployment <deployment-name>

**Fix**:

- Use kubectl describe deployment to see why it's stuck.
- Check if pods are failing (see Pod Issues above).
- Use kubectl rollout undo deployment <name> to roll back.

## Scaling Doesn't Work

**Likely cause**: Resource limits too tight, or HPA misconfigured.

kubectl describe hpa <name>
kubectl get pods -o wide

**Fix**:

- Check limits and requests in pod spec.
- Make sure Metrics Server is installed and running.

# 4. Service & Network Issues

## Service Not Accessible

**Check if:**

- Pods have the correct labels (match selector)
- Service type is correct (ClusterIP, NodePort, etc.)
- DNS name resolves

kubectl get svc
kubectl describe svc <svc-name>
kubectl get endpoints

**Fix**:

- Ensure pod labels match service selectors.
- Use kubectl port-forward to test locally.

## Ingress Not Working

kubectl describe ingress <ingress-name>
kubectl get pods -n ingress-nginx

**Fix**:

- Check if Ingress Controller is installed and running.
- Look at annotations and path rules.
- Make sure DNS is pointing to the right IP.

# 5. YAML Errors

## Apply Fails

kubectl apply -f file.yaml

**Fix**:

- Use kubectl apply --dry-run=client -f file.yaml to test config.
- Validate YAML with kubectl explain or a linter like Kubeval.

# 6. Cluster Cleanup & Debug Tools

## Useful commands:

```
kubectl get events --sort-by=.metadata.creationTimestamp
kubectl get pods --all-namespaces
kubectl top pod
kubectl delete pod --force --grace-period=0 <pod-name>
```

## Tools That Help

- stern: live tail logs from multiple pods.
- k9s: terminal UI to manage Kubernetes.
- kubetail: tail logs from multiple pods.
- kubectl-debug: run a debug container in the pod's namespace.

www.ingramcontent.com/pod-product-compliance
Lightning Source LLC
LaVergne TN
LVHW051538050326
832903LV00033B/4307